THE MONEY MANUAL

THE MONEY MANUAL

Another great book by Award-winning Author, Dr. Christine Topjian

Christine Topjian Publishing

CONTENTS

DEDICATIONS		vii
Introduction		1
Glossary		4
1	Your Relationship with Money	8
2	Tithes & Offerings	19
3	Good Debt vs. Bad Debt	29
4	Credit Cards	36
5	Fees, Fees, Fees & Interest, Interest, Interest…They ARE Bad	40
6	Real Estate and Investments	43
7	Little Ways To Save More of Your Money	52
END OF BOOK NOTES		59
ABOUT THE AUTHOR		67

| v |

DEDICATIONS

This book is dedicated to my dad, Dr. G. Topjian who instilled in me an excellent understanding of money and finances from a young age.

I pray that this book goes a long way in helping each person who picks it up learn and know more about their finances in an effort to get them on their way to a healthy or healthier financial future.

Finally, thank you for picking up this book.

Introduction

Money.

We all have a relationship with it.

Some have a great relationship with it, while others don't. Having a great relationship with money means that you understand your income and expenses, you know and have consistent income to cover your expenses and then some, that you know exactly what is happening with your investments and generally, that you are fairly financially literate. Is this an exhaustive list to have a great relationship with your money? No, but it's a great place to start.

If you identify yourself as one who doesn't have a great relationship with it, consider this your invitation to start building a great relationship with it.

Why? Because we all need a certain amount of money to live and to support ourselves (but I'm guessing that since you've picked up this book to read or at least to peruse, that you already know that). :)

No matter how old or how young we are, we all have a relationship with money and we all need some money, if not for luxuries, then we need it for basic food, shelter, clothing and other basic needs (think Maslow's hierarchy of needs).

The best way to have the most solid relationship with money is to understand money and how it works. And turning to the wisest written source of all is also very important. Turn to the Bible to teach you what you need to know about money.

Money is an energy. You can bring more of it into your life by following specific steps and actions or you can cause it to leave your pocket or your bank account quite quickly never to return if you don't understand how it works.

ANOTHER GREAT BOOK BY AWARD-WINNING AUTHOR, DR. CHRISTINE TOPJIAN

This book is intended to teach you how money works and how you can increase your chances of keeping that lovely paper in your wallet, bank account or pocket for longer and by increasing the amount you already have in there.

This book goes a step further than other books in that it explains Biblical concepts and tools for acquiring, working for, bringing money into your life and how to protect the money you have while also making sure to increase the amount of money you have.

> To begin with, there is a mindset we need to take off the table: money is not hard or impossible to get.

To begin with, there is a mindset we need to take off the table: money is not hard or impossible to get. Money is just like anything else - it needs to be worked on, it needs to be respected for what it can do for people and at the same time, we need to avoid the unnatural love of money. I will explain that last point further: money can do some wonderful good in the world but it can also do lots of bad. Examples of bad include such things as purchasing drugs, using it for unlawful uses, using it to bilk people out of their savings, using it for human and sex trafficking and such. Money can be used for those things but certainly shouldn't be.

This book will teach you to have a great relationship with your money and to do lots of good with it. In order to do that, I have provided you with reflection activities, concepts and time to step away from this book and to think and reflect about money. We don't have a great relationship with anything unless we consistently work at it. Yes, consistently. So that means that when you're done reading this book, that's not the end of it. You still need to work at it, read up about money, real estate and savvy investments, you need to make it a part of your daily life. Just like with fitness or anything else, it doesn't just happen. We need to work on it consistently.

In this book, we will also be referring to Scripture in an effort to understand how *God provided* this resource and how He wants us to use this resource in an intelligent, strategic and sustainable way. Many people erroneously think God doesn't care about how much money we have or that it's wrong to want more. I can't tell you how wrong that line of thinking is. True, not everyone is called to be a money mogul and some people are called to more modest living (and there isn't anything wrong with that), but to not have a good understanding of money, how it works and how to protect and grow (at least a bit) the money we do have, is unwise.

Get ready to enjoy and please, when there are exercises to be done, please do them. They will help solidify your understanding, they will help you relate the concepts taught back to your life, they will have a big role to play in helping you better understand and eradicate any and all limiting beliefs you have about money. So please, do each exercise and enjoy the process.

In an effort to help you right at the onset, I have also included a glossary of some helpful financial terms that you would benefit from knowing. It would be wise for you to take some time and study the terms, put in alpha order for your benefit, and to test yourself every now and then to make sure you remember what the terms means. I know some of this may seem daunting at first (almost anything is when you first begin) but it is important and worthwhile to study and to review to grow your knowledge and money literacy today and going forward.

Please also feel free to enjoy the benefits of our online community where you can share, receive support and talk with others (in kind and respectful ways, of course) at drchristinetopjian.com.

Thanks and happy reading, writing, reflecting and learning.

Glossary

Asset: any property owned by a person or company, regarded as having value and available to meet debts, commitments

Accounts Payable: (usually abbreviated as A/P) the money a company owes its suppliers for goods and services that have been provided and for which the supplier has submitted an invoice. (This makes accounts payable different from accrued expenses, which do not have invoices to match.)

Accounts Receivable: (usually abbreviated as A/R) the money a company's customers owe for goods or services they have received but not yet paid for. For example, when customers purchase products on credit, the amount owed gets added to the accounts receivable.

Bonds: a bond is a type of security under which the issuer owes the holder a debt, and is obliged – depending on the terms – to repay the principal of the bond at the maturity date as well as interest over a specified amount of time, with interest

Capital: the capital of a business is the money it has available to pay for its day-to-day operations and to fund its future growth. The four major types of capital include working capital, debt, equity, and trading capital.

Capital gains: the increase in a capital asset's value and is realized when the asset is sold. Capital gains apply to any type of asset, including investments and those purchased for personal use. The gain may be short-term (one year or less) or long-term (more than one year) and must be claimed on income taxes.

Cash Flow: is a real or virtual movement of money, such as when a person makes a payment for something, the person receiving the money gets an increase in cash flow (cash money to be used).

Credit Limit: the maximum amount you can charge on a credit account, such as a credit card. As you use your card, the amount of each purchase is subtracted from your credit limit. And the number you're left with is known as your available credit. Credit limit amounts can vary widely and usually, the more payments you make on time and in full and the greater your credit score, banks and financial institutions will give you greater and higher credit limits.

Credit Score: generally ranges from 300-850, and the higher your number, the better you look to a lender because it signals that you're more likely to repay the full amount owed.

Debt Consolidation: is a form of debt refinancing that entails taking out one loan to pay off many others. This commonly refers to a personal finance process of individuals addressing high consumer debt

Dividends: payments made by companies to their shareholders based on the number of shares they own. Dividends are usually paid when a company has excess cash that is not being reinvested into the company. This excess cash is divided up among shareholders and paid out to them.

Expenses: the cost of operations that a company incurs to generate revenue. As the popular saying goes, "it costs money to make money." Common expenses include payments to suppliers, employee wages, factory leases, and equipment depreciation.

FICO: is a company that reports credit scoring for individuals.

Fixed Interest Rate: is an unchanging rate charged on a liability, such as a loan or mortgage. It might apply during the entire term of the loan or for just part of the term, but it remains the same throughout a set period.

Investments: the action or process of investing money for profit or material result.

Liabilities: a thing for which someone is responsible, especially a debt or financial obligation.

Offerings: a contribution, especially of money, to a Church. This is over and above what you pay as tithes.

Portfolio: a range of investments held by a person or organization. Usually a "balanced" portfolio means that a person or organization has a range of investments and diversifies their portfolio (a.k.a. The proverbial not putting all your eggs in one basket).

Return on investment: is a performance measure used to evaluate the efficiency of an investment or compare the efficiency of several investments. People generally look for investments that have(or that they feel may have) the highest return on investment.

Stocks: a share which entitles the holder to a fixed dividend, whose payment takes priority over that of common-stock dividends.

Tithes: a one-tenth part of something, paid as a contribution to a religious organization or compulsory tax to government.

Variable Interest Rate: is a rate that fluctuates with the market interest rate (known as the prime rate) and is usually stated as prime plus or minus a percentage amount. For example, a variable rate could be quoted as "prime - 0.8%". So, when the prime rate is, say, 5%, you would pay 4.2% interest (5% - 0.8%).

Write-off: is a reduction of the recognized value of something. In accounting, this is a recognition of the reduced or zero value of an asset. In income tax statements, this is a reduction of taxable income

1

Your Relationship with Money

Every person has a relationship with money, whether they realize it or not.

Money is a thing, an object, and so each person has a relationship, active or inactive, dormant or vibrant, positive or negative, with that object. When we realize that money is an object that can flow freely and easily into and out of our lives, we begin to realize that there are things we can do to bring money into our lives, and conversely, there are things we can do to take money out of our lives.

No matter what industry you work in, what position you are in, where in the world you live, whether you are a tenant or a landlord, whether you are BIPOC or white, or any other factors, this concept applies to you.

> It doesn't matter whether your family is very well off or extremely poor - you can set your own money blueprint and be led by the Holy Spirit to increase money and wealth into your life. It's as simple as that.

When we think about money and about receiving money positively, when we spend time with the Holy Spirit in focusing and visualizing the receipt of money and when we work smart, money begins to flow into our lives. Why would we do this? Well, I'm pretty sure most people (myself included) enjoy it when money is flowing into their life – this means that we not only have enough money to pay our bills, but that we also have enough left over for disposable income to enjoy responsibly.

When we spend time with the Holy Spirit in visualizing money incoming and the receipt of good news and good wealth, and we do so in gratitude, it will begin flowing into our lives. I myself was skeptical about this for a time and so I began putting the concept into practice. As a result, I opened up new income streams for myself and accordingly, tithe more as well.

It doesn't matter whether your family was or is very well off or poor - you can set your own money blueprint and be led by the Holy Spirit to increase money in your life. It's as simple as that.

Practice Exercise: I'd like to give you an opportunity to put this into practice. Set aside about 15 minutes in your day to visualize and think about money flowing into your life. I will give you a 5-point step by step guide on how to do this. Just try to make sure you have 15 uninterrupted minutes to put this into practice.

Step 1 - Get into a quiet place and sit comfortably. Turn off all distractions and close your eyes (I find this works better with eyes closed.)

Step 2 - Begin to get a very clear picture in your mind of either a cheque having been written to you or money having come into your bank account.

Step 3 - Focus carefully and take your time in seeing every detail. You can spend time seeing the cheque being written in your name in the "Pay to the order of" part, and seeing the cheque signed and the amount you would like to see on the cheque. If you prefer an interac e-transfer, see your bank account having increased in the amount the Holy Spirit is guiding you to.

Step 4 - Hold the image in your mind carefully, seeing every aspect of it, even feeling the check between your fingers or feeling the phone between your fingers and the app showing you the increase in the amount. Feel it and enjoy the feeling of that new money being in your possession.

Step 5 - At the end of the 15 minutes (put a timer on if you wish), slowly come back and re-open your eyes. Don't jerk yourself out of this visualization but come out of it slowly.

Congratulate yourself for taking the time to do this and thank the Holy Spirit for guiding your visualization so beautifully. After all, the Lord is the One who is going to make this happen for you in His time and in His way.

Prayers

There are many people who have turned away from prayers to God. Prayer is a very powerful tool that helps bring good blessings (yes, money included) into your life. The Lord has ways to bring money & wealth into your life that you have not thought of - and the beautiful part is, you don't have to think of the ways all on your own. All you have to do is pray and let the Holy Spirit guide you. Once you have prayed, being mindful and attuned to the promptings of the Holy Spirit is very important.

Biblically, we have been given every tool to bring blessings of all kinds into our lives and we know that Scripturally, the Holy Spirit is there (once you have been baptized) to come over you and to speak to you, to guide you on how to increase blessings in your life. I will provide an example: when a woman named Mary was looking to bring money into her life (she was looking to bring many blessings into her life but because this is a book on money, I will focus on that part of her prayers) so she began praying for it. Through her prayers, and in her quiet time alone with Jesus, the Holy Spirit began speaking to her and she felt compelled to take a closer look at her finances. As it turned out, Mary realized that the investment vehicle she had put her RRSP money in were not doing much for her in terms of a return on investment (that key term is in the glossary above) and on top of it she was paying the bank a management fee to invest her money so she was really not getting anything significant as a return. She therefore decided to learn about investing and how to carefully and cautiously invest her money in different investment vehicles. She began making a healthier return on her investment and she stopped paying the bank's fees. She was already seeing a really good turnaround.

We can see in the above example that Mary's relationship with money was growing and improving and that she was beginning to take a much greater role in securing her financial future.

Practice Reflection

Ask yourself: What is my relationship with money? Do you have a good relationship with money or one that really needs to be improved?

ANOTHER GREAT BOOK BY AWARD-WINNING AUTHOR, DR. CHRISTINE TOPJIAN

Do you feel your money management skills are pretty good, very good or do they need improvement? Jot down your responses in the space provided and then keep reading on in the book to learn more about money management. Following your readings, review your responses in this section and see if you would still answer the same after learning all that you do from this book.

_____
_____
_____
_____
_____
_____
_____
_____
_____
_____
_____
_____
_____
_____
_____
_____
_____
_____
_____
_____
_____
_____

Any Relationship Needs Work

As the heading indicates, any relationship is going to need work and consistently so. You cannot, for example, expect to be a great wife or husband after one conversation with your spouse. You also cannot expect to be a Doctor after one day of medical school. You need to work on your relationship with money and if you think about it, it is one of the most significant relationships of our lives.

> Our relationship with money is one of the greatest constants in all of our lives so if we don't know how to make that relationship work, then we are doing ourselves a disservice that will impact ourselves, and the next generation of family members after us.

Our relationship with money will evolve many times in our lifetime and hopefully, will grow and improve and become more solid over time. You will know your relationship with money is improving when some or all of the following happen:

- The number of books, articles and resources about money is increasing and you know you are actually reading, taking notes on and carefully considering the teachings you are reading
- You start to notice that you are understanding more and more when you see, hear and read concepts about money being talked about on television, in the news, in magazines, etc.
- You realize that you are paying (more) attention when the bank or financial institution sends you paperwork, documents and reading materials

- You realize that when the bank or financial institution sends you updates, you begin to look at things more critically and evaluate whether that change now really works for you
- Your own financial vocabulary is growing
- You have (and use) more investment, banking and money apps on your phone or devices
- You are able to contribute ideas, opinions, facts and stats significantly when conversations arise about money and finances in social settings
- You start to build your own repertoire of experience so that when you hear someone else talking about an aspect of finance, you are able to intelligently and in a well-researched way, support or refute what they are saying and can back that up with supporting evidence
- You start to understand (or better understand) market trends and analysis
- You feel more confident paying your bills because you know you are more financially literate
- You are able to more strategically make intelligent and informed investment choices and decisions
- You are able to see through unnecessary and avoidable costs & expenses when they arise
- You are better able to do your taxes each year and you can much more easily understand how to factor in your expenses versus your income each year

Understanding the way money works and how to make money work for you is a tremendous feeling. It's a great feeling to know how you can make sure you are doing all that you can do to secure your financial present and future, and it's a great comfort to see that God, through the Holy Spirit, is behind you, helping you make the best and most informed financial decisions.

Some Prayers

I'd like to suggest some prayers that you can use to not only help you achieve a great relationship with your money (both the money you already have and that which you will have) today and every day.

Remember, we were never meant to do this on our own. God has given us all the tools we need to go to Him and to make the best and most informed financial decisions and when we make good, solid & well-informed financial decisions, not only do we win but all those around us win. How so? Because when we do well, we are in a better position to bless and share with our loved ones, as opposed to borrowing from our loved ones.

Prayer to better understand money:

Lord, I pray for You to help me understand what my current relationship with money is and how this can be improved. I ask You to speak to my heart and to show me where I have and am going right and wrong when it comes to managing my money. In Jesus name. Amen

Prayer to steward your money (more) wisely:

Lord, I pray for You to help me steward the money You have given me more wisely. Show me how I should be using my money, how I should be investing my money and how I can be a wiser manager of money. In Jesus' name. Amen

Prayer to increase money in your life:

Lord, I ask You to show me how I can improve my relationship with money so that I can increase the money coming into my life. You already know my finances, every penny in my bank account and You know my expenses and my dreams and desires. I ask You to speak to my heart and show me how to increase the money coming into my life. Please speak to me clearly through the Holy Spirit on how I may do this, and consistently so. In Jesus' name. Amen

Prayer to understand what tithing is and to proceed in paying your tithes:

Lord, I understand that there is such a thing as tithing mentioned many times in the Bible. I ask You to teach me and show me what tithing is, how it is relevant today and how I am supposed to engage in it, if it is something You wish for me to be engaged in. In Jesus' name. Amen

Prayer to ensure that you are paying your tithes to the right place(s):

Lord, I pray for Your help and Your wisdom to help me ensure that I am paying my tithes to the right institutions. You know what each institution is doing and You know which institutions follow You faithfully. I pray that You show me by speaking to my heart and let me know to whom I am to pay my tithes so that they can do the maximum good for your Kingdom. In Jesus' name. Amen

Prayer to get a better sense of how, where and with whom you should be investing:

Lord Jesus, I pray for You to show me how, where and with whom I should be investing my money. I pray for You to guide my investment decisions so that I am able to get the most money and returns on my investment. Show me, Lord, how these ways and these places are the right ways to invest my money, because this is ultimately Your money, I am a steward of Your money. In Jesus' name. Amen

Prayer to better understand stocks, bonds and investment vehicles:

I pray, Lord Jesus, for You to bring me a much better understanding of stocks, bonds and investment vehicles. I pray for You to bring me the right books, resources and websites so that I can better understand how all of these investment and money-making vehicles work. Give me the mind to understand and to see how I can strategically apply the concepts in the right ways. In Jesus' name. Amen

2

Tithes & Offerings

Within Scripture, we are provided with many tools to help us achieve financial prosperity. These Scriptures are your road map. They are your road maps to understand major prosperity and to understand how God's system of wealth works. You happily and cheerfully provide the set amount of a minimum of 10% and then He will pay you back manifold. Here is one Scripture that refers to this:

> Malachi 3:10 (NIV)
> Bring the whole tithe into the storehouse, so that there may be food in my house. Test me in this," says the LORD Almighty, "and see if I will not throw open the floodgates of heaven and pour out so much blessing that you will not have room enough for it.

Many people go through life expecting financial abundance and there is nothing wrong with that. We just need to make sure that we are working hard and strategically to acquire that financial abundance.

Following God's given road map is the surest way to do this. This means following these steps:

1. Pray about where or to whom you should be paying your tithes
2. Pay your tithes with cheer (not begrudgingly)
3. Ensure the payment has been made successfully
4. Wait for your return to be provided

1. Pray about where or to whom you should be paying your tithes

I want to spend a bit more time on this point since it is very important. Most organizations would be happy to receive your financial support (at least, I can't think of too many that wouldn't). But not every organization qualifies. The organizations that qualify are the ones that honor Jesus and specifically uphold Biblical values. I see some Churches and religious organizations that call themselves Churches, but they do not uphold Scriptural teachings. As such, it is so very vital to pray first about the organization and whether they are truly in-line with Christ. Scripturally (in Matthew 24:5), Jesus warns "For many will come in my name, claiming, 'I am the Messiah,' and will deceive many.'" These are organizations that are masquerading as being "with Jesus" but are far from implementing Scriptural teachings.

A personal recount: I was considering paying tithes to a certain Church, not because I felt particularly connected to them or really felt that they had provided me with invaluable teachings but because I was such a new born again believer and I didn't know any better. A friend advised me of the same thing I am advising you to do here: pray about the institution before you donate to them. So, I did. I got into a quiet space and asked God if this was the right place to whom I should pay my tithes. The sense that I got immediately was a resounding "no!" I was a little bit confused because I thought (like many others) that a Church is a Church. Not so. When I dug a little more and researched and spoke to some patrons (and former patrons) of the Church, little by little I began to see that this was not the right place for me to be fonating because they were actually misguiding and misleading people. I instead chose (after praying about it) to donate to another Church, one where multiple people assured me were well in-line with Scriptural teachings and where we could clearly see God's Scriptural teachings being upheld.

2. Pay your tithes with cheer (not begrudgingly)

When you pay your tithes with cheer, you are fulfilling your Scriptural responsibility. We are not supposed to pay begrudgingly but with joy. Why? Because we know that we are doing a good thing and helping and supporting the Kingdom and its purposes.

If you are one who sometimes has some difficulties paying with cheer, try to get into the habit of cheering out loud when you pay your tithes. Literally. Cheer out loud. This will help ensure your joy when you are doing this.

3. Ensure the payment has been made successfully

If you are making the payment by cheque, you can request a confirmation of receipt once your cheque has been received and/or processed. If you are paying online, check to ensure that the payment went through successfully, by looking for the confirmation email following payment. If you are paying by credit card over the phone, it's a good idea to wait until the rep confirms that your payment has been processed.

Of course it is necessary to look for the confirmation that the payment has been successfully processed in order to have ensured that your tithes have been paid.

4. Wait for your return to be provided

Many people are under the impression that their return will be provided instantly. This is not usually the case. We will usually have to wait patiently as God sets things up so that we can receive our return. It is a good idea and totally fine to pray for God to speed things up and to bring you your return more quickly as well as to open your eyes for when you do receive it. I have seen many people who have tithed successfully and when they receive their return, they didn't recognize it as such and so they assumed that they did not receive it. Therefore, pray for Him to open your eyes and to show you when you have received your return.

How Much To Give

One of the great things about tithing is that you only give from income you have already earned, not income that you don't yet have. Scripturally, it is the first 10% of the money you have earned, so if you have earned $1000, then you pay $100 or more.

The word tithe literally means 10 in Hebrew. In Leviticus 27:30, it says, "A tenth of the produce of the land, whether grain or fruit, is the Lord's, and is holy." And Proverbs 3:9 says, "Honor the Lord with your wealth, with the first fruits of all your crops." Now, at the time of this writing, many were farmers and so it refers to crops. We are meant to extend that today to any profession or work that you are engaged in.

The first 10% applies to any and all income, including passive income from such things as stocks, bonds and real estate.

So, a wise thing to do would be to take the pay that you have received and to immediately pay a Christ-honoring organization the 10% or more to ensure you have made your tithes payment. Trust me when I say (because yes, of course, I have paid my tithes too) that while it can hurt the flesh a little bit because we as humans don't sometimes want to give away money, it is what we are called to do for the good of all and it is the way to much greater wealth.

Documenting Your Income and Your Giving

I highly recommend to anyone to record your income for yourself and record your giving, including what date you are giving and the exact amounts. This will help as a reminder of the blessings you have received and will help you realize that you are doing right by paying your tithes of 10% or more.

Memories can get fuzzy over time and so writing these things down is very beneficial.

A Man Who Grumbled While Paying

I saw a man many years ago who gave more than the 10% but did so with such a negative attitude. In conversation with him, I asked him what was the matter. He had mentioned that he knew he had to give away the 10% but that he hated doing it. I asked him why he hated it so much and he said that while he had seen the Lord bless him extremely abundantly, that he still hated giving because the amounts kept getting bigger because his income was growing. I gently reminded him that

God likes a cheerful giver and helped him pray to have the strength and the presence of mind to be a cheerful giver. Today, he is a much happy giver and he writes down all the ways (both financially and non) that God has blessed him in his gratitude journal. This has also been a fantastic gateway for him to realize the good that the money he donates has done for others.

Focus on the Benefits

I want to talk about this point just a little more. I know how difficult it can be to pay one's tithes. I get it. I've been there. One thing that helps me to do this is to remind myself of all the good this money is doing. For example if you are tithing, it is likely that you actually have a relationship with God. What I like to think of is how God's will is being furthered here on earth and how I am helping to create abundance and provide support for others, in the name of Jesus. Some of the ways that I am doing this (and that I know others do too) is by helping homeless people and providing them with food, shelter and clothing, providing safe spaces for runaways and battered people, providing financial resources and outreach abilities to Churches who are looking to reach more people who don't yet know Christ, providing housing for orphans and people who are in need, and by providing outreach help services for those who find themselves scared and unexpectedly pregnant, among others.

In other words, I focus (and try to help others focus) on the good the money is doing, how it is helping others and how it is enriching the lives of others. Tithing should not only be about increasing our own wealth and financial well-being.

What's An Offering Then?

We often hear the term tithes and offers. We've talked about tithes as being the first 10%. What is an offer then? It's the extra. After you have given your 10%, the offering is anything you voluntarily give over-and-above that. So, if you have paid your 10% and then you also decide to bless someone or an organization with an additional amount given, that is considered your offering.

Do I Have to be Christian to Tithe?

This is a great question that I get asked a fair bit. Does one have to be Christian to tithe? Will a payment of tithes be invalid if I am not a Christian or a born again Christian? When you give to God (a Christ-honoring organization) it is never for nothing. Of course you will still be blessed as a result of it and God will see the good you are displaying that flows from your heart. Remember, He knows you better than you know yourself, so He knows exactly what you are doing and the intention with which you are doing it. Another important point to make here is that tithing isn't a way to earn God's love—because *we already have it*. In Matthew 23:23, Jesus warns against focusing too much on the rules of tithing without paying attention to the more important things like justice, mercy and faithfulness.

How the "Paying Back" Could Happen

Many people pay their tithes and then expect new money to fall into their laps right away. It doesn't really work that way. We need to pay our 10% cheerfully and then we need to wait.

Financial prosperity and this "paying back" can and will happen in different ways for different people. Here are some ways I have heard financial abundance manifest for some:

- A leak happened in the basement home and insurance covered it completely, allowing for a newly renovated space
- A student won and was granted a financial scholarship for the entire of their program
- A relative passed away and left a sizeable sum to the person
- A new job presented itself and the person was able to make much more money and become much more financially comfortable
- A client finally paid a business' bills and because they made them wait a longer period of time, they paid them with interest (which was never part of the initial agreement)
- A worker received verbal and written praise at work along with a sizeable raise in pay
- People who unexpectedly received money from someone or somewhere
- A free item drops into your lap
- The Lord brings to your attention how your investments could be bringing you a much better return if you do the following steps
- You receive a sizeable discount on something

You may notice that for some of these events, they didn't start off as very positive. Taking the first example of a leak in the basement, I don't know of too many people who would consider that a good thing. But God brought good out of a bad situation. He brought good out of an unfortunate happening and blessed the person with it. God is always able to bring good out of something bad.

Stay in Faith

One of the most important things we all need to do when we are waiting for that financial abundance is to stay in faith in Christ. It can be really difficult to part with one's money no matter at what point in time in your life or in the economy it may be, but we need to put our faith and our trust in God that He will bring good things to us, and that includes paying us back and blessing us financially for the tithes and offerings we have paid.

Another thing that is so helpful in your waiting is to pray. Pray for God to give you patience, understanding and for Him to purify your heart if you know or feel in your heart that your reasons for giving were impure. Here is a suggested prayer for this (of course, you are welcome to change the words, edit or add to this prayer to make it more authentic to you) but you are advised not to take out the last words: In Jesus' name. Amen. Why? Because when we pray, we are praying on the highest and most noble name that exists: that of Christ. We are humans and we are sinners so we cannot pray in our own names.

Lord Jesus, I pray for You to help me by revealing to me if my heart needs purifying. You know me better than any person and so I ask You to show me and tell me if there is something unclean in my heart. Help me be a cheerful giver of tithes and offerings so that Churches and organizations that honor You and do Your will have the resources to do all that they need to. Help me be a pure giver and then also, help me wait patiently and in good cheer for my financial prosperity. In Jesus' name. Amen

Tithing While Being in Debt

This is an important point to mention: should we still tithe if we are in debt? The answer is yes! It doesn't matter how much or how little money you currently have. Even if you are in debt, the Lord will bring you the money you need to get out of debt once you have tithed with whatever you have. He will bring you all that you need to get out of debt and to step into financial prosperity, and because He is God, He can do it while you are giving any little you may have and paying your tithes with that little. In Mark 12:41-44, we are presented with an old woman who gave all that she had left: Then a poor widow came along and put in two small copper coins. Jesus teaches the disciples that the woman gave more than the rich. The poor woman, as a widow, would have had no source of income after her husband's death. Therefore the two small copper coins were all she had - and yet she offered them to God. Don't think that this woman was not in turn, also blessed.

There are many examples of people who have been in debt but still stayed faithful and gave. The Lord saw their goodness, obedience, faith and blessed them in return. Even if your income is $100, tithe with the $10 and see how the Lord blesses you in return.

3

Good Debt vs. Bad Debt

There is such a thing as good debt, just as there is such a thing as bad debt. People often lump these two together as "debt is just bad" but that is not the case. There are some forms of debt that are actually good to have while bad debt is definitely something each person should try to discipline themselves to reduce and then to eliminate as quickly as possible.

Good debt is an investment in something that creates value or produces more wealth in the long run. It also adds value to your equity (meaning, your total financial worth) such as a home. Examples of good debt include:

- a mortgage on a home
- a student loan to pursue education for a career
- a loan to launch a business

Now, some people look at a mortgage as good debt and that's good, because it is. But one thing we have to keep in mind is that for any debt you have, you must be able to afford the payments. Not being able to afford the payments will mean that you will likely eventually default on the debt. In the case of a property, you will lose the property if you cannot make the payments consistently. Some banks and financial institutions will provide a small grace period window but once that grace period comes to an end, they will be expecting their money to be paid.

Bad debt is debt taken on to buy something that immediately goes down in value or to buy something that you can't repay on time and in full, thus incurring interest charges and more debt. Examples of bad debt include:

- charges on a store credit card at a high rate of interest
- a personal loan to pay monthly expenses
- or anything you don't really need or that you cannot afford to pay

We all really need to be mindful of our spending and only purchase things we know we will be able to afford. For example, yes, a mortgage is considered good debt but if you have purchased a $5 million home and you know your income and possible rent (if you decide to rent it out) received will not cover all of the following: your monthly mortgage payments, your tax payments, and possible monthly maintenance fees (if you live in a condo where maintenance fees are applied) then that would also be considered bad debt because you are likely to default on your mortgage loan. To default (just to repeat this because it's a really important point) means that you are unable to pay the amount owed in full and therefore you don't make the payments, that is called going into default and the lending company will come and take the property away from you.

Bottom line: You have to be able to comfortably afford the entire purchase price.

Credit card debt is also one of the greatest traps people fall into. More on that in the next chapter but this is a really important point and I highlight it because many people don't initially realize that they can't actually afford either the purchase in full or the high interest on the card. I should say here that every credit card has a very high interest limit, meaning that if you are even one day late, they will charge you a very high rate of interest. Imagine having that interest compounded over several months and we are getting into very ugly financial scenarios. We want to avoid this at all costs.

Your Mindset

When asked why they got into a debt situation, many people will explain that their parents or guardians were in debt and it's always sort of been something that the family took on. I will never forget a lady my mother was talking to who kept complaining "We're in the red, we're in the red. We cannot make any of our payments anymore and my husband keeps buying." Taking on debt (any kind) needs to be a conscious, well thought-out decision that is made after good and careful consideration. The payment requirements will not stop coming just because you don't have the money to make the payments.

Some people are also of the mindset that if they can just make their minimum monthly credit card payments, that that is enough. Not so.

For example, if you owe $5000 on your card and the minimum payment is $100 and you make only the $100 payment, that does not mean you are now in the clear. Good rule of thumb: If you can't make the entire payment at once or in installments with 0 interest, then you can't afford it right now. I know it's not some peoples' favorite thing to hear (and I have myself had to gulp hard when I realized that a purchase

I wanted to make was unlikely) but we have to have enough presence of mind, maturity and forethought to ask ourselves whether we can really afford the item.

If now is not the right time to purchase it, make a plan for additional income and map out when you might likely be able to purchase it. It will be much more satisfying as well when you realize you actually have the money to purchase something outright without going into debt for it.

> Your mindset when it comes to money and spending is so important. The wrong mindset could lead you down a road to debt that may be extremely hard to recover from.

Your mindset when it comes to money and spending is so important. The wrong mindset could lead you down a road to debt that may be extremely hard to recover from. Those little purchases and "treats" you get yourself are great, but you need to be careful with those too because too many of those little "treats" and you could be putting yourself in a very difficult financial position.

At a social function once, people were talking about how they enjoyed treating themselves to this purchase and to that high-priced item every now and then. When we started talking about it in more detail, I discovered that their "every now and then" was very frequent and that they were wasting large sums of money. People can sometimes forget that those little items can really add up quickly and that we can find ourselves in an undesirable financial situation at the end of the month when we realize we have spent more than we intended to. It can be pretty unpleasant if we see that we need to dip into our savings in order to cover those "every now and then" items, worse yet if we don't have the money to pay for them, we can land ourselves in some hot water.

Some items that you should likely limit because they can carry a hefty price tag can include:

- Regular cab or such rides
- Food delivery (taxes and delivery tips in addition to the already high cost of store-bought food)
- Take out food instead of making food at home
- Grocery stores that are exceptionally expensive
- Not using coupons when they are available
- Buying the higher priced brand option when a lower priced and more economical option is more reasonable and available
- Buying an exceptionally expensive car when you know the payments will be a stretch for you at this time
- Exceptionally expensive vacations
- Trips to the hair salon when you could (learn to) color your hair and highlight your hair on your own
- Doing your nails at home (home mani-pedis are very underrated)
- Buying lunch or dinner from outside every day (even fast food buying will add up very quickly)
- Not being careful about stocks and portfolio investments which could cause you to lose your money pretty quickly
- Not paying attention to the interest rate on your credit card and only making the minimum monthly payments
- Going to restaurants frequently (you are paying the restaurant's profit on the food and drinks, paying for the taxes and hopefully a kind and appropriate gratuity for the server)
- Always buying your books, magazines and reading resources when you could get them from the library

I think you get the idea of where I am going with all of this. The bottom line is that we all need to make financially wise and sound decisions and that comes with knowledge, financial literacy, and financial maturity. It is never too late to start to become financially literate and to know and understand how money works, the income that is coming in and the money that is going out. Keeping a tally of this (even if you have an accountant or financial advisors) is so important. Do so on your phone or other device so that you can keep track of your spending.

Practice Exercise:

Take a moment right now and reflect for yourself on how carefully you are managing and spending your money. Are you partaking in any or all of the items in the list I mentioned above? Do you believe you need to curb your spending a little bit or do you believe that you are being financially wise? If you are being financially wise, can you do an even better job?

Remember, being honest with yourself right now will be tremendously important to your tomorrow and the tomorrows of your family and friends. Why? Because they will watch you and they will be inclined to follow your example of fiscal responsibility. Whether we like to admit it or not, we are largely influenced by our environment and so we do pick up lots from those around us. Use the space provided below for your answers:

_____
_____
_____
_____

THE MONEY MANUAL

4

Credit Cards

This is such an important topic, it deserves its own chapter. Why do I say that? Because people often forget what expenses they put on their credit card and they often forget to check their expenses list when it comes time to pay their credit card debt each month. In addition, the super high interest rates that credit card companies charge is no laughing matter. The fees are high and yes, if you are even $1 less than the full amount, you will be subject to paying that super high interest rate on the $1.

According to an article by CNBC dated May 2022, US credit card debt hit an all-time high of $930 billion with younger Americans having the highest delinquency rate. According to an article in the Globe & Mail in April 2022, Canadians are piling on credit card debt again. This year's debt is a significant increase from last year, according to Stats Canada, at 8.9% increase.

Credit card debt is often out of sight and out of mind. It can be (and is) very easy & tempting to swipe our card, make the payment and just walk out of the store with your new purchase in hand, completely forgetting that we just incurred that amount and that we will have to pay for that later.

If we really think about it, credit card debt can become a monstrous worry and can sneak up on you very quickly. Let's take the example of a pair of shoes: we see a beautiful pair of shoes on sale for $250 and we decide we can buy it, so we do so. We charge it to our card on, say, April 2nd. We go ahead and we enjoy the shoes and the compliments that may ensue from wearing them. Then, on May 1st when we get our credit card statement, we realize that it's time to make payment on those shoes, except that we may have overextended ourselves this month and we can't afford to pay for the whole thing at once. The minimum payment is $10 so we make that minimum payment, perhaps feeling good that we made a payment. We may not be paying attention to the fact that we are now paying 32% interest that the credit card company is charging on $3000 (the $250 is included in that $3000) so we are now paying $956.80 ($2900 - $10 payment we made) in interest alone. As you can see, this can add up very quickly and so we need to be mindful and cautious each time we slip that credit card into the merchant's credit card machine.

The Credit Check

Another item that is important to mention with credit cards is that in order to get and to qualify for that credit card, the company does a check into your credit rating. Each time they do this, it actually lowers your credit rating.

There are some websites, such as credit karma, where you don't get dinged for the check and some places accept this credit score and report instead of TransUnion or Equifax. Mind you, not all places accept credit karma because it is not a full and complete report on what you owe.

Does Making My Payments In Full and On-Time Increase My Credit Score?

The simple answer to this important question is yes. People who are financially savvy know that each time they make a credit card payment in full, they do increase their credit score. Increasing your credit score is, of course, a great thing to do and really simply, a smart way of using the credit card but you need to make the payment in full and on time each and every month to reap the advantage of that. So, as in the amount in the previous example, you would need to pay off the entire $3000 in its entirety and by the due date.

HIGH Interest

It isn't a secret that the interest rate demanded and imposed by credit card companies is exceptionally high. It also isn't an accident that this is not exactly printed on the card itself. If it were, it would serve as a very helpful and effective reminder to the person using it that they are opening themselves up to a high debt amount each time they use the card and don't pay off the full amount by the due date.

Annual Credit Card Fees

Another important point to talk about is the high annual credit card fees you have to pay just to hold a company's credit card. Personally I find annual credit card fees ludicrous and the only card in my wallet is the one that has 0 annual fees. Companies charge this over-and-above the ridiculously high interest rate and they state that they use these payments to help cover the costs of the facilities, the materials, the customer service reps and more. Frankly, it's as if they don't make enough money off of the high interest rates but if people will pay the annual fees, they will keep charging them. The way to encourage companies not to charge those fees is by stopping to use their card. Simple as that. This is another example of fees adding up. If your card charges you an annual fee, ask yourself if your credit card is really that advantageous and if you want to keep it.

5

Fees, Fees, Fees & Interest, Interest, Interest...They ARE Bad

Most banks and financial institutions (also referred to as FI) are notoriously good at charging fees for everything. They charge fees for account set-ups, usage, they charge you a fee to leave your money with them, they charge you fees to invest your money for you and more. We need to be mindful of the fees we are incurring because like any other expense, they do add up quickly and we will be responsible for them each month. There are also some banks and FIs that allow for "all inclusive" banking which means that if you keep a certain amount in your account all the time, they will waive the fees. This can get tricky, though, because if you are a person that makes frequent transactions, you may at any point in time easily dip below the threshold amount and then they will usually ding you with a fee of (around) $29.95 or more.

In addition, banks and FIs always say that the fees are subject to change at any time and will normally send out emails to notify clients of this. When you get these notices, it is a good idea to pay attention to them. They are letting you know their fees (therefore, your expenses) are increasing. You can then see if it is still beneficial for you to hold onto that account with that institution.

Being Mindful

Being financially savvy is just a matter of being mindful. Mindful how? Mindful about our money, where it is going, where it is coming in from and how we are using the resources we have been given and more. Sure, almost anyone you ask will be happy to take more money, but ultimately, we need to be good managers of the money we already have.

It has been stated previously that even people who won the lottery and got huge influxes of money soon (or fairly soon thereafter) lost it because they were not managing the money properly. That's the thing about money - it's all about how you manage it, not always just about how much of it you have coming in. I also note here that when we have much, giving away to the right charities and organizations will be beneficial. It will mean your tithes amount will have increased and you can offer more and your charitable donations are tax-deductible so each donation lowers the amount of tax you pay.

A Last Word About Fees

When companies and professionals bill you, don't just take their word for it. Check the math yourself. Check the bill yourself and make sure everything is adding up properly. Companies will at times add little fees and interest charges here and there that you may not even be aware you are paying. If you were not late with your payment, why would you pay their interest fees? What do you do if that happens? Call the company or the entity that billed you and ask them about it. I recall one time when this happened to me (it's happened way more than once but I'm giving you one of the examples) with a utilities company. There was a less than $5 charge on my bill but I saw no reason for the charge.

It didn't make sense. As such, I called the company and the customer service rep said that it was related back to the old bill that had such-and-such balance. I pointed out that that bill was paid in full and on time, so I challenged the interest charge. She didn't know how to answer me. Instead, she kept me waiting for over a week to get the final answer of "You're right, ma'am, you should not have been billed that interest charge." We sometimes erroneously believe that these companies don't make mistakes. They are human like us and they do and so we need to be watching where our money is going.

6

Real Estate and Investments

How you invest your money is very important. Many people are of the frame of mind that either they don't have enough to invest or they go in full throttle and invest every penny they have without having taken the time to educate themselves on financial literacy and what, say, the history of that investment vehicle is. There are many investment vehicles available to all of us but they are not all created equal, nor do they all provide the same benefits.

Here are some of the investment vehicles available today:

- Real estate (apartments, condos, townhouses, semi-detached houses, full detached houses, house boats, etc.)
- Stocks
- Bonds
- Crypto
- GICs

Of course, the costs and risks associated with each can be quite different. Real estate, for example, asks for a significant up-front investment and then if you play your cards right, you can make money each month from renting out your home (if that is the direction you want to take with that investment). If you get enough in rent, you can have a little left over each month after paying your mortgage, taxes, maintenance fees (if there are maintenance fees) and repair expenses.

Generally speaking, real estate is usually a good bet (especially in Canada) where the values of homes pretty consistently increase unlike in some other places where the values of homes can dip so much that your home ends up being worth less than your mortgage, but you're still stuck with your mortgage.

Stocks can be a good bet depending on which ones you choose and choosing the right stocks should not be left to chance. You will want to pick stocks where you understand the way that stock behaves and you are ready for the stock to go up and go down in value over time. It is not typically the case where people get rich quick with stocks - they are more so an investment vehicle you use and benefit from over time.

The most guaranteed investment vehicle there is, is a GIC. This is a bank-backed investment vehicle where you earn little interest but your principal (the original amount you put down) is guaranteed (which means you will definitely get your initial investment back).

Educate Yourself

The frank fact is that you need to take the time to educate yourself over time and to learn about money, and investments and how each behaves over time. I can't tell you how many times I have been in social situations where people are asking another about which stock they think they should invest in, meanwhile that person was and is speculating as much as the person asking. I'm not saying don't talk to people about their investments to learn more and to see what they're doing, I'm just saying don't jump on the proverbial bandwagon and buy up this stock or that one just because someone you spoke to said that they think it's a good stock. At the end of the day, you will be the one making or losing your money if you don't invest wisely and over the long term.

Taking classes and educating yourself does not need to be very costly. Sure, there are many programs out there that are very expensive. Why do you need those? I have learned all that I know from reading books from the library, praying about the stock and letting the Holy Spirit guide me, from watching instructional videos totally free of charge and from reading up a lot about the company, its values and its stated direction.

I will never forget many years ago when I was enrolled in a weekend seminar course to have an intro to stocks. The weekend was meant to wet your appetite so you end up buying a much longer course that was so much more expensive. I learned a fair bit in the weekend course and knew that I needed to take the time to take the information away and to process it slowly and at my learning pace. A LOT of info had been thrown at us (that's not a bad thing) but I knew that if I didn't take the time to review the information, to practice the concepts and to gain a greater handle on it, that nothing else was ultimately going to stick. I chose to do that while others in the course decided to opt into the longer and more involved course which cost several thousands of dollars. When the learning facility held a reunion day where we could all discuss and see our progress, in my conversations with others, I found that none of them had continued with investing, even after having spent thousands on the longer course. They all (no exceptions) said that they could not dedicate any more time to doing this and that they didn't feel confident and comfortable enough to continue. To this day, I read on my own, watch more educational videos, pray over any investments I make and I always do as the Lord guides with investments.

God Has No Place?

Some people may not understand why I would involve God and the Holy Spirit in a book about investing. It's really quite simple. Nobody wants better for you than God does. We were also never meant to do investments (or life) independently from Him. As such, we need to always go to Him in prayer and to ask Him if this is the right avenue or if another one is. We should never assume that we know better than Him and that we don't need Him on a topic as important as our investments.

How do we know what He is guiding us to do? We have to pray about it and we have to be still so we can get a sense of what He is saying, how the Holy Spirit is guiding us. If we have already made investments independent of the Holy Spirit, we need to ask if we have done the right things and if not, what needs to be done. One of the many great things about God is that even when we have done something outside of His will and it has been wrong, He always gives us an opportunity to fix the situation. He gives us a way out and never really leaves us alone to fend for ourselves.

> One of the many great things about God is that even when we have done something outside of His will and it has been wrong, He always gives us an opportunity to fix the situation. He gives us a way out and never really leaves us alone to fend for ourselves.

Automatic Easiness

When I was first beginning my process of learning the investment landscape, I had read a book from a so-called guru who said that automating one's investments is the best idea. Years later and with much more experience under my belt, I can tell you that that is not the best advice. While we should definitely know what we are paying for and should keep on top of when our payments are due, automating things takes mindfulness out of the equation. I used to do that and turned around years later and realized that because I wasn't paying very close attention to the investments (just letting the automated thing happen) that I wasn't looking for or paying attention to better strategies that had now become available and from which I could have benefited from. Because I had automated the process, I didn't look carefully at the fact that I now had saved enough money to double up my payments, for instance.

When you are a savvy investor, you know that on Monday, this payment is being made to meet this debt and that on Friday, you are going to be receiving this income from that source. Automating your investments causes you to stop thinking actively about your incoming and outgoing money and that's not always the best course of action. I respect that everyone is busy and that people have many things to do but this is your money, your family's money and likely your nest egg investments - you cannot leave all of that up to automation over the long term.

Just Start

I want to be clear about this point: just start. Start learning, start reading, start understanding, start getting a handle on your money, start asking the right questions, start taking ownership of your money and start learning about the best investment vehicles for you. You will see that as you do this, your relationship with money will grow and will improve significantly. Just as in class, when you understand something, you tend to enjoy it a whole lot more. Just as in class, when you ask questions and you have a great teacher who can answer those questions for you very clearly, your enjoyment level and your involvement increases because you realize that you are "getting it." And that's a really cool thing.

Said differently, many people think understanding money and investments is a big huge mountain that they cannot even fathom climbing. Or they think that the mountain of debt they may be facing is a big huge mountain they don't even want to think of because they feel they will never get out.

These are not great ways of thinking about things.

Even if you are under a mountain of debt and you feel you will never get out or if you have bills coming in and interest rates adding up and collection calls coming in, start tackling the problem, not running away from it. The more you run and avoid the problem(s), the worse the problem(s) gets. When you begin to confront the problem, you begin to see that slowly, with time and with effort and with little payments here and there, things start to get much better. As you begin to wade in the pool of better money management, you will see how much better you will start to feel about all of it and you will eventually begin to see the light at the end of the tunnel.

Creditors Usually Want to Help

The thing creditors want most is to get paid. They will often even settle for a little bit less if they know that they will be getting something. It is for this reason also that I say to begin making your payments, and maybe you can negotiate better deals and better rates. It's when you run away from the problem that things will get worse.

Overestimate Costs

A last word in this section on investment: overestimate your costs. This means that when you foresee a cost coming, overestimate it and set money aside to cover that cost. It may end up costing a bit more or a bit less than what you had estimated, but if you overestimate the cost, you will not find yourself in a very tight situation. If the cost ends up being as you thought it would, then great, you estimated correctly. Here are a few examples of what I mean:

- A gentleman investor was about to purchase a house and offered to put down a certain percentage. Because he had other real estate investments, the bank only asked him to put down the minimum amount. He instead decided to set aside more than the required amount and on the day he was supposed to make that payment, he went ahead and put down much more than was expected. The bank was unpleasantly surprised (when you put down more, the chances of you paying it off more quickly tend to rise, so the bank makes less money) and he ended up paying off the house much more quickly than he thought he would have been able to.
- A woman was about to take on a loan from her line of credit in order to start her business. She had estimated that the costs involved with the startup would be around $30,000 so she used this method and she overestimated that she would need about $35,000 for her new business. While we need to watch our expenses (for sure), this lady knew that business costs can sometimes be pretty unpredictable so she overestimated the amount that would be needed so that she wouldn't run into unforeseen costs later on.
- A mechanic had just purchased a new space for his mechanic business. As with all new builds, it takes the government some time to determine the exact and actual square footage of the

space, which means your maintenance fees (which are charged per square foot) can go up significantly once the final square footage has been properly assessed. During his purchase of the property, property management had estimated the monthly fee to be at $750. The fee that was ultimately assessed was over $900 per month - quite a significant jump. Needless to say, the mechanic was quite disappointed at this development.

- When Dan was preparing for his family's annual vacation, he knew they were on a budget but he also wanted something nice for his family. As such, Dan began price comparing hotels, seeing what promotions and coupons would be available for the destination, and began talking to family, friends and co-workers about how he could afford the destination of his family's choice while also keeping to their budget. His budget was a healthy one and he decided to begin to find little ways of staying within it, such as preparing and packing their own lunches, renting a car for only part of their stay, and more cost-cutting measures. He began to find wonderful and relatively non-cumbersome ways of staying within budget, and he was able to provide a wonderful vacation for his family within the set generous budget.

- Stan was waiting for his monthly credit card bill to come through. He knew that he had been good this month and had not overspent but he was trying to find ways to make sure he stayed within a reasonable amount. He also knew his mortgage payment was coming up right around that time as well as a family birthday so he had three big payments to make. Because he wasn't sure how much each of the three items would cost, he overestimated each. When he got his bills, he could see that overestimating had been the right thing to do. He owed a little more on each than he had thought but he had more than enough to pay them each because he had set aside more than he thought he would need.

- Preparing for a big birthday dinner for his wife, Dennis knew he was going to invite 50 guests to their home for his wife's birthday surprise. As he wanted to make it a lovely evening with champagne, hors d'oeuvres, soft music and an elegant affair, he still knew he had to keep his eye on his budget since they had a growing family. Dennis chose to make it a lovely and lavish affair, while still keeping in mind his budget and making sure to spend but not overspend. Instead of a completely catered event, he ordered take out and put the food into lovely serving platters himself, instead of serving staff, he hired some students from his classes to serve during the course of the evening and when it came time to presenting his wife with a vacation, he purchased it at a time that was not top of season and got a great deal with his air miles points.

What am I saying with all of this? Life adds up. Things get expensive. So, wherever possible, overestimate your costs and find ways of cutting unnecessary expenses so that you can be sure you are not stuck with unpleasant financial surprises later on. There are always ways of being smart with your finances.

7

Little Ways To Save More of Your Money

Taking a critical look at your money and your expenses is no small or easy feat. It is an important and critical task and you need to take it seriously. I am not saying don't spend money, don't enjoy life and be cheap. Far from it. I am saying to enjoy your money, enjoy life and be smart about your expenses and your finances.

> Enjoy your money, enjoy life and be smart about your expenses and your finances.

There are always ways we can cut our costs. Whether your bank account is quite plentiful and healthy or you are not in the most secure place with your finances at the moment, there is much you can do to lower your costs and your expenses. The following list gives you some quick-and-easy tips and tricks to get more from your dollar and to cut your expenses. Remember, this list takes into consideration a variety of people from parents with children to singles to younger adults and more who may have picked up this book and are looking to learn and to be more mindful about their finances. The following is not meant to be an exhaustive list but it is meant to be a starting-off point so you can begin thinking in this way. Of course, when you are reading through the list and inspiration for some cost-cutting methods hit you, jot them down in the notes section in the back of this book or take your phone or device and jot them down. You can always save the notes for later and come back to them, making minor or major tweaks to them as you go.

Enjoy the list:

- Make your own morning coffee or latte at home and take it with you in a travel mug
- Make your own lunch and your family's lunch so you don't have to buy food from outside each day
- Make food on the weekend and pack it away so you will definitely have dinner ready to go for during the busy week
- It's great to go get your nails and hair done every now and then but you can try to cut those costs by using groupon deals or doing your own hair and nails. Getting hair dye from the local beauty supply or a drug store will work great too
- Recycling your clothes and wearing outfits in different combinations more than once
- Save on that gym membership and set yourself up with a super effective and inexpensive home gym that you don't have to get in the car or on the TTC and go to - it's downstairs in your home or in one of the rooms in your living space
- Cutting coupons at the grocery store is a great money-saving tactic and definitely worth your time in searching out the coupons
- Using the app flipp.com to compare the prices of groceries at different grocery stores so you can get your groceries for the cheapest price available

- Instead of using ride companies, try the TTC - it's a great chance to be environmentally more conscious, save money from the car, the insurance and the gas and gives you a chance to get outdoors and enjoy the fresh air
- Buying your family's groceries from a warehouse type store like Costco instead of a smaller grocery store
- Invest in kitchen gadgets so that meal prep will be easier and cheaper, causing you to be less likely to go out and buy take out or even worse, go to restaurants
- Use economy brand detergent
- If massages are not covered by your insurance provider, consider only getting 1 massage per month as opposed to more
- Pay attention to when gas prices are lowest and fill up at that time
- Walk more places instead of using your car or vehicle
- Sell items around your home that you don't need anymore
- Avoid expensive clothes shopping trips and either wear your current clothes again or shop at less expensive places like Walmart, Byway or the Bay
- Bring your own bags when grocery shopping - you'll save 5 cents per bag
- Check over your utility bills to see where you might be wasting money (ex. Doing laundry after 7 pm which is off-peak hours is very economical and you still get your laundry done)
- Pick up a part time job
- If your children go on field trips, maybe as a family you can set a limit to go on a certain number per year as opposed to going on all of them
- Carpool or rideshare so your kids can get to school on time and safely and it's not always you who has to drive them in your own vehicle
- If you currently subscribe to many magazines or streaming services, maybe identify the most expensive one(s) and cancel your

subscription to that or those. You would still have the other ones that are cheaper to enjoy
- Wait for sales and clearances to buy all that you don't need to buy right now

Costs add up. Savings also add up. Take a careful look at your expenses and see where you can save money and cut spending. Your pocketbook will thank you as will your bank account. It benefits you significantly to be wise (not cheap) and mindful with your money and to learn how to manage your money carefully.

> It doesn't matter if you are 15 or 45, start today.

It doesn't matter if you are 15 or 45, start today. Start managing your money little by little today. If you feel you are getting tired or frustrated, set it aside and continue tomorrow but stick to it. Money management does not just happen in one day, it is a life skill that you need to master because our relationship with money doesn't really ever end. And if you are like most, you'd like to live comfortably and leave some for the next generation.

A Great Legacy

One of the best legacies we can leave our children or our families is that of a healthy financial nest egg. No, it doesn't mean we have to be cheap all our lives and be penny-pinching. I don't ever recommend that. I recommend being smart and savvy with your money, having great sources of income and doing all you can to help your money grow.

If you're not sure how this can be done, pray about it. Let the Holy Spirit guide you. Let Him show you how (much more) financially savvy you can be and how much more you can do to help yourself and your family. Don't forget that when you are smart with your money, you are taking a financial burden off of your family because they won't have to worry about supporting you financially, they will know you can take good care of yourself.

Financial savviness is not just for doctors, lawyers, accountants and such professionals. It is for everyone and everyone should partake. Everyone should be financially literate and know and understand how money works and most importantly, how to make it work for them. With respect, those in banking are not going to be staying up at night worrying about your wealth and your finances. They are up worrying about their own so please do not rely on them to show you the right way. I'll share an example about this: as I was reviewing my own finances years ago, it dawned on me that I had missed out on a money-saving opportunity that I qualified for due to Covid and would have saved me a nice amount of money. When I asked my accountant about why he hadn't mentioned it to me, he simply said (somewhat callously) that it wasn't his job to point those things out to me but to work with the givens I provide him. That's when you know you're not working with the best and reinforces that you need to look out for you.

Practice Exercise:

Monthly Expenses
So, take some time right now and review your monthly expenses for the next 5-6 months. Make a list of all your variable and fixed expenses and write them all down. If you're not completely sure about the exact amount, put in your best overestimate of what it will be. Then, begin

to devise ways of reducing each expense, whether that means you are going to start doing laundry in the evening, shopping at a different (less expensive) grocery store, going to pick up the food yourself instead of having it delivered and paying delivery fees and tips, buying your books secondhand for school or getting them from the library and many more things you can do.

ANOTHER GREAT BOOK BY AWARD-WINNING AUTHOR, DR. CHRISTINE TOPJIAN

_____
_____
_____

END OF BOOK NOTES

Use this section of lines to make all the notes you would like, to jot down thoughts, ideas and reflections. Use it as you see fit and in ways that work for you.

END OF BOOK NOTES

END OF BOOK NOTES

END OF BOOK NOTES

END OF BOOK NOTES

END OF BOOK NOTES

END OF BOOK NOTES

END OF BOOK NOTES

ABOUT THE AUTHOR

Dr. C. Topjian is a Doctor of Ministry from Christian Leadership University and lives in Toronto, Ontario with her family. She is an Award-winning author, performer & producer, and deals in Toronto residential real estate. You can read more about her, access other books and resources and join our online community at DrChristine-Topjian.com.

www.ingramcontent.com/pod-product-compliance
Lightning Source LLC
Chambersburg PA
CBHW072106110526
44590CB00018B/3333